IMAGES
of America

CHICAGO'S
FORGOTTEN SYNAGOGUES

IMAGES
of America

CHICAGO'S
FORGOTTEN SYNAGOGUES

Robert A. Packer

ARCADIA
PUBLISHING

Published by Arcadia Publishing
Charleston SC, Chicago IL, Portsmouth NH, San Francisco CA

Printed in the United States of America

Library of Congress Catalog Card Number: 2007930865

For all general information contact Arcadia Publishing at:
Telephone 843-853-2070
Fax 843-853-0044
E-mail sales@arcadiapublishing.com
For customer service and orders:
Toll-Free 1-888-313-2665

Visit us on the Internet at www.arcadiapublishing.com

Anshe Kanesses Israel (Men of the Israel Assembly) was built in 1912 and was located at 3411 West Douglas Boulevard. It was though to be the largest synagogue on the West Side. It was known as the Russisher Shul as most of its members emigrated from Russia. During the early part of the 20th century, The rabbi at Anshe Kanesses Israel was Rabbi E. Epstein. (Courtesy of *History of the Jews of Chicago*.)

CONTENTS

ACKNOWLEDGMENTS

About four and a half years ago I started my research on Chicago's forgotten synagogues. I published my first book, *Doors of Redemption: The Forgotten Synagogues of Chicago and Other Communal Buildings* in 2006. This book was a contemporary look at what happened to the hundreds of Chicago synagogues and communal buildings over the past 150 years, with interviews with members going back 100 years. It was a nostalgic look back at Chicago synagogue history.

I have selected from this group those photographs that would be of interest and that accurately portray Chicago synagogue life. The book is divided by neighborhoods, which I thought would be a benefit to the reader. It would take a book many times larger than this to fully show the depth and breadth of Chicago's Jewish synagogues and institutions. I hope that this book will spark a feeling of the old memories of what Chicago's Jewish community created over the past 150 years as well as new interest to this generation.

I would like to thank the following individuals and organizations for working with me to create this book, and without whom this could ever have been accomplished. Dr. Irving Cutler, who contributed many photographs and who gave of his time; Norman Schwartz's classic photographs; and Steve Grubman, who contributed his photographs of synagogues that have been torn down. To the Meites family through Thomas and Jerome Meites, whose grandfather's book on Chicago Jewry, *History of the Jews of Chicago*, was vital to this effort; to Rabbi Rallis Wiesenthal, who contributed photographs of synagogue memorabilia and translated many synagogue names; and Mort Einhorn, who contributed photographs from his father's collection. To A.G. Beth Israel; Anshe Emet, Bob Krakowsky; Beth Iztchock, Malke Rine Baskt; B'nai Abraham Zion; B.J.B.E.; B'nai Zion, Helen Stopek, Harvey Gold; History Museum; Chicago Sinai Congregation; Ida Crown Academy, Rabbi Leonard Matanky, Wendy Margolin; Indiana University, Charles W. Cushing Collection; Jerome and Joan Drapekin Collection; Mike, Express Printing of Wheeling; Jewish Community Centers; Julia Johnas, Gail Juris; Temple Judea Mizpah, Terry Kane; Temple Beth El, Vicki Mackay; Temple Beth Israel; Temple Emanuel; Ner Tamid; Rodfei Zedek; Mary Jo Doyle; and Spertus College of Judaica, Chicago Jewish Archives, Joy Kingsolver, Jacqueline Jackson. Thanks also to Barbara Chester, Betty Cohen, Trudy Levenstam Cooper, Saraine Levenstam Corn, Honey Deitch, Sidney and Raymond Epstein, Chester and Naomi Gaynes, Rita Stevens, Ruth Schultz Hecktman, Charlotte Kaplan, Sarane Meyers, Sheryl Zisook Schneider, Shirley Gould, Allen Sared, June Sochen and Jean Uhlmann.

A special thanks to my editor at Arcadia Publishing, Melissa Basilone, who help shepherd this project through a tight schedule and the demands of publishing. Finally, I would like to thank my wife Fern Abrams Packer, who endured my absence for many months, and whose help, critique, and good humor brought this book to completion.

INTRODUCTION

Chicago synagogue history is very much the history of Chicago. It is a story of changing neighborhoods and demographics, of people and institutions and how they reflect who we are and what we hope to be. Immigrants looking for a new and better life, whether white or black, Jewish or gentile, or Muslim or Buddhist, or European, Hispanic, or Asian our shared values and basic needs are the same.

The fact is that in the first part of the 20th century over 75 percent of Chicago Jewry lived within the city, to the reverse in the second half of the century where over 75 percent of the faithful lived in the suburbs, and barely 25 percent lived in the city of Chicago. This ever-changing and ongoing metamorphosis continues down to this very day. While some Jewish congregations are barely surviving in the urban setting, many others are not only surviving, but thriving with renewed commitment to the social and religious need for these institutions.

This book covers approximately 150 years of Chicago synagogue architectural history in photographs and historical vignettes. In this case, it is different from my first book in that the emphasis then was on more contemporary photographs with accompanying interviews from members whose lives I chronicled. It shows how literally hundreds of synagogues, schools, and communal buildings have evolved into African Baptists or Hispanic Pentecostal churches as wells as Asian Temples and Mohammedan Mosques.

As neighborhoods change, as one indigenous population was supplanted by another, we see in their religious architecture, the early promise (of their expectations) from one generational immigrant group to another.

The fact that all life revolved around the synagogue or communal building (social, educational, and religious) tells much about what earlier generations invested in the meaning of these places and of their faith and the emphasis placed on community.

I am an example of, and possibly the last of, that generation that truly understood how the synagogue was the epicenter of neighborhood life. (Much like a boys and girls club defines the center of life in a secular sense.) Although I speak from a "Jewish" perspective, it is interchangeable with any other group, faith, or immigrant class in that it represents an "everyman" who can relate to this experience. I was born in the 1950s and came of age in the turbulent 1960s. My family's movements echo that of entire generation of immigrant Chicagoans, from the Near West Side of South Wood Street and West Washburn Avenue in the first decade of the 20th century, to the greater west side prior to World War I where they prospered, a short stay in Humboldt Park and onto Rogers Park on the Far North Side in the mid-1950s. All along the way, they left behind tangible landmarks of their cultural-religious institutions in each neighborhood they lived in.

By the mid-1950s in Rogers Park I went to public school five days a week, followed by Hebrew school (four days a week, Friday night Sabbath services, Saturday morning youth services, and finally Sunday school). To say that B'nai Zion of Rogers Park was the center of my life and that of my family and friends would have been an understatement. But I was not alone; I was quite typical of the youth of my generation. We saw nothing strange in this commitment. It was not that we were so faithful or religious, it was a much larger idea than we were, it was as much social as it was faith. I guess you could say it was just the thing to do and be (we really did not question our parents' authority as much as the youth of today, or at least our parents never let us question it). The commitment to our synagogue was a "fait accompli," it just was. It was a fact of life rarely questioned, I said rarely.

Finally, this book will illustrate (despite) the ever changing dynamic of synagogue and neighborhood, the continuity of synagogue and community from city to suburbs. From Congregation Ner Tamid (conservative) in west Rogers Park to Congregation B'nai Emmunah (conservative) in Skokie, which merged with Beth Hill (conservative) in Wilmette, from Congregation B'nai Zion (conservative) in Rogers Park merging with Shaare Tikvah (conservative) of North Park to Temple Mizpah (reform) in Rogers Park merging with Temple Judea (reform) in Skokie, the ever changing, ongoing process of evolving synagogue congregations of aging and rebirth. The closing or merging of these synagogues is a natural process that has been evidenced over the past 150 years and will continue as long as we feel the need to change where we are and where we feel we should be. We are not a static people, on the contrary we are very dynamic and we react to our situations and environment. In some instances, we do wither and die, but for the most part, we are active participants of our lives, not passive bystanders.

One

NORTH SIDE

This photograph was taken at B'nai Zion in 1955 at Friday night Sabbath services in the main sanctuary.

B'nai Zion (children of Zion), at 1715 West Lunt Avenue in Rogers Park, was built as St. Paul's by the Lake Church and was bought by the congregation in 1918–1919 and outfitted as a synagogue to serve the growing Far North Side neighborhood with a new, modern, and progressive form of conservative Judaism. The first full-time rabbi was Abraham L. Lassen who served from 1919 to 1949. (Courtesy of the Rogers Park/West Ridge Historical Society.)

B'nai Zion, the oldest conservative Jewish congregation in Chicago, established in 1919, built their magnificent synagogue at 1447 West Pratt Boulevard laying the cornerstone in 1928; the dedication was in 1929, just before the Great Depression. The longest serving rabbi was Abraham L. Lassen, 1918–1949. It is seen here as it appeared in 1976. (Courtesy of Steve Grubman.)

Rabbi Henry Fisher was the second-longest serving religious leader of Congregation B'nai Zion. He was called to the pulpit in 1949.

In a photograph taken in the 1950s in B'nai Zion's Oliff Auditorium, the Hebrew school children take part in the annual Purim festival.

This is how the main sanctuary of Congregation B'nai Zion looked in 1963 after a major renovation was undertaken to update the house of worship. Notice the deep, highly polished wood paneling. (Author's collection.)

The photograph shows the changing face of the East Rogers Park community. The last remaining synagogue had to sell its community center building to raise funds to replace an aging infrastructure; consequently it was sold to Lake Shore Nursery Schools, which later purchased the main building. (Author's collection.)

The front entrance and lintel of B'nai Zion Synagogue is seen here. (Author's collection.)

The *VOICE* of Congregation B'nai Zion

The Rabbi's Study

When some worshippers come to the High Holiday services, they question what a strange thing we are doing. Let us imagine that we had to explain to a visitor from another planet, just what it is that is going on here. What could we say except that on the High Holidays, Jews all over the world gather together in big empty rooms to talk to someone who isn't there. The one who is not there, we call G-d. Two people stand up in front of the group and lead in chanting and explaining the prayers. The one who chants we call the "Chazen". The one who teaches and explains the prayers, we call the "Rabbi", and then of course the alien would say, "Take me to your Reader."

There are many worshippers who are not sure what they are doing in the synagogue and not at all sure that they believe a good deal of what is going on. The old irrelevant words in our prayers, G-d, organized religion. They are not at all sure, they have their doubts. In order to quiet the doubts, we must make Judaism count. Judaism teaches creativity and change, personal autonomy and freedom. We teach that when old traditions no longer point the way when we need to go off into unchartered territory, it is up to us to create new relevant traditions.

(continued on next page)

HIGH HOLY DAY SCHEDULE

SELICHOT SEVICES
Saturday, August 27   10:30 PM
Social Hour hosted by Sisterhood
in Oliff Auditorium   9:00 PM

ROSH HASHONASH 5755
Monday, September 5   8:00 PM
Tuesday, September 6   8:30 AM
Wednesday, September 7   8:30 AM
Three Pulpit Flower Arrangements by:
Gary Freeman in memory of his beloved Father , Cantor Harold Freeman.
Mrs. Miriam Perlman in memory of her beloved husband, Leo.
Betty Packer and Family in dearly beloved memory of Jay C. Packer, Abraham and Rose Rubinstein and David and Ida Packer

YOM KIPPUR
Wednesday, Sept. 14 (Kol Nidre)   6:30 PM
Thursday, Sept. 15   9:00 AM
    Ne'ilah   5:00 PM
    Closing Shofar   7:15 PM
Three Pulpit Flower Arrangements by:
Sidney Saperstein in memory of his beloved parents Abraham and Esther Saperstein.
Mrs. Bea Tucker in memory of her beloved Husband, Louis, and her beloved daughter, Charlotte.
Betty Packer and Family in dearly beloved memory of Jay C. Packer, Abraham and Rose Rubinstein and David and Ida Packer

SUKKOT
Tuesday, Sept., 20,   9:00 AM
Wednesday, Sept., 21   9:00 AM
Pulpit Flowers hosted by Helen Stopek in memory of her beloved Husband Harry Stopek

SHEMINI ATZERET
Tuesday, Sept., 27   9:00 AM
Yizkor Services and dedication of plaques
Tuesday, Sept, 27   7:00 PM
    (Erev Simchat Torah)
Pulpit Flowers hosted by Helen Harris in memory of her beloved Husband Alvin Harris

Rabbi and Mrs. Kleinman will host an extended Kiddush. Everyone is invited.

SIMCHAT TORAH
Wednesday, Sept., 28   9:00 AM
Community Services in the Singer Sanctuary in celebration of the Joy of the Torah.
All Ages are Welcome!

The *Voice* was the newsletter of Congregation B'nai Zion. Newsletters were the most popular form of communication in the religious communities, often heralding the news of the changing fortunes of the community and members. (Courtesy of Congregation B'nai Zion and Helen Stopek.)

The **VOICE** *Of* Congregation B'nai Zion

JULY 26, 2002   AV 17, 5762

THE LAST ISSUE OF THE "VOICE of Congregation B'nai Zion"!

On Sunday, July 21st, a very moving ceremony took place in the Singer Sanctuary. A Torah was being donated to the Ethiopian Jewish community in Kiryat Gat, Israel and dignitaries from JUF were there to accept it. Rabbi Michael J. Schorin passed the Torah to Rabbi Ira Udovin, who will personally bring the Torah to Israel.

On Sunday, June 30, another Torah was given to the new Congregation Shaare Tikvah B'nai Zion in a ceremony beginning at the B'nai Zion building, then going by bus to the Shaare Tikvah building. Members of the two synagogues accompanied the Torah to its new home where the ceremony was continued.

As this is being written, stained glass windows are being removed from the sanctuary, the memorial boards are being taken down, and all items going to the new Congregation Shaare Tikvah B'nai Zion are being prepared and packed for moving on Monday, July 29, 2002. The closing date for the sale of the Sanctuary building to the Lake Shore Schools is August 1st.

Our thanks go to Beverly Tatz of the Ritual Committee for seeing to it that all ritual and Judaic objects that will not be going to Congregation Shaare Tikvah B'nai Zion have found appropriate sites where they will be truly appreciated and used. Beverly was also responsible for all the historic material and memorabilia to be given to the archives of the Chicago Jewish Historical Society which is housed at Spertus Institute. Todah rabbah.

To make contributions in memory or in honor of someone, call the office at Congregation Shaare Tikvah B'nai Zion, (773) 539 2202.

Editor's note: This will be the last VOICE of B'nai Zion. But you can look forward to receiving Koleinu, the voice of Shaare Tikvah B'nai Zion.

YAHRZEIT CONTRIBUTIONS

Donor	*in beloverd memory of*
JACK COHN	mother, Naomi Cohn
NAOMI GAYNES	father, Abraham Blank
NATALIE R. LIEBERMAN	
	father, Dr. John J. Rayman
BRUCE SHAPIRO & SARA KANDERLAN	
	Rose Shapiro

OTHER CONTRIBUTIONS

SARAH & SIDNEY BLUMEN, in beloved memory of Sam Slavick;

BETI & HASKAL BROCINER, in honor of Betty Packer's birthday, and in honor of the marriage of Eddie Blumen and the marriage of Dara Shifrin;

SHERRELL FELLERMAN, in beloved memory of Sam Slavick;

SUNNY & SHERMAN KATZ, in beloved memory of Sam Slavick and in beloved memory of Eleanor Friedman;

MITCHELL PADNOS FAMILY, in beloved memory of Sam Slavick;

ROSE & BEN SAITLIN, in honor of the marriage of Eddie Blumen and in beloved memory of Sam Slavick;

SHIRLEY SLAVICK, in beloved memory of husband, Sam Slavick;

HELEN STOPEK, in beloved memory of Sam Slavick.

B'NAI ZION FAMILY

Mazel Tov to:

SARAH & SIDNEY BLUMEN, on the marriage of son, Dr. Edward Blumen, to Pat Foran.

YETTA SHIFRIN, on the forthcoming marriage of granddaughter Dara Shifrin to Lee Bass September.

****

BEREAVEMENTS

SAM SLAVICK, long time member of B'nai Zion and beloved husband of Shirley Slavick.

This is the last newsletter of Congregation B'nai Zion after 84 years in the Rogers Park neighborhood and nearly 75 years on West Pratt Boulevard. With a dwindling, but valiant group of members, many going back to the very beginning, B'nai Zion was forced to sell their beloved sanctuary, later merging with North Park's Congregation Shaare Tikvah (gates of hope) on North Kimball Avenue. (Courtesy of Congregation B'nai Zion and Helen Stopek.)

Congregation Beth Sholom (house of peace) was established in the Rogers Park neighborhood in 1938. It was the first and leading traditional synagogue in the community. The building was renovated in 1952 to a more postmodern look in keeping with the upscale East Rogers Park area. Rabbi Elimelech Beige, Rabbi Jacob J. Nathan, and Rabbi William Gold were their long-serving spiritual leaders. In the 1990s, a large fire killed plans for a major rebuilding effort. The building is slated to be torn down. (Author's collection.)

This photograph is of the Beth Sholom Hebrew school. (Author's collection.)

16

This is the current look of the Congregation Beth Sholom in a photograph taken in the late 1990s. (Author's collection.)

Congregation Beth Sholom's edifice is to be torn down soon. (Author's collection.)

Congregation Kesser Maariv was one of the leading orthodox synagogues in the Rogers Park community. The official name is Kesser Maariv (crown of the west or western crown) Beth Hamidrash Hagdol Kesser Maariv Ante Luknik (house of study, western crown men of Luknik) and was located at 6418 North Greenview Avenue. The heralded West Side congregation has its roots in the Maxwell Street community. It later moved to the West Side and another group moved to the South Side. This structure was built in about 1955. The beloved Rabbi Zev Wein was the spiritual leader for many decades. After years of vandalism, the congregation moved to Golf Road in Skokie. (Courtesy of Norman D. Schwartz.)

Congregation Beth Israel Anshe Yanova (house of Israel, men of Yanova) was established on the West Side and moved to the Rogers Park community in 1955 during the wave of change in Lawndale. It was located at 1328 West Morse Avenue. The building was originally the Co-ed Theater. It was a traditional synagogue. Its last rabbi was Bernard Perlow. (Courtesy of Irving Cutler.)

Congregation Beth El of Rogers Park was established in the 1930s in this brick three-flat building located at Rogers Avenue and Sheridan Road. Their long-serving religious leader was the beloved Rabbi Jacob Pikelny. The congregation was in existence for over 30 years, until Pikelny passed away in 1969 and the building was sold to a day care center. (Author's collection.)

Congregation Sinai of Rogers Park was housed in a converted mansion and was located at 6905 North Sheridan Road. This old established orthodox synagogue was led by Rabbi Romirowsky for most of its existence. The synagogue closed in 1989 and was sold to a developer; today a group of luxury town houses is on the site. (Courtesy of Norman D. Schwartz.)

Rabbi Jacob Singer poses with a Temple Mizpah confirmation class. (Courtesy of Temple Judea Mizpah and Terry Kane.)

The Temple Mizpah's confirmations class poses with Rabbi Silverman in 1949. (Courtesy of Temple Judea Mizpah and Terry Kane.)

VOLUME 30 NUMBER 6   19 CHESHVON 5723   November 16, 1962

PLANS SET FOR RALLY DINNER DECEMBER 2

Regular Sabbath Services

FAMILY WORSHIP SERVICES

Friday, November 16, at 7:45 PM

At this service, members of the Ninth Grade will assist the Rabbi with the reading and the Kiddush and Torah service.

Rabbi Buchler will tell a story-sermonette:

"BETWEEN THANKSGIVING AND CHANUKAH"

Children whose birthdays fall in October or November will be called to the altar for blessing and will receive a token gift from the Women of Mizpah. Members of the new Tweens group will serve as ushers at this service.

REGULAR SABBATH SERVICES

Friday, November 23, 8:15 PM
Rabbi Buchler will preach on:

"THE REAL TRAGEDY IN DEATH: AN IMPORTANT LESSON FOR LIFE"

The Haftarah teaches us much of life and death, in the moving elegy which David recites for Saul and Jonathan when they have fallen in battle. But the sorrow for which David weeps is not the real tragedy of Saul's death. There is much more about his life about which to grieve. But David does not then understand. We should, and the lesson is one about life -- not death.

At this service, we shall celebrate the

BAR MITZVAH OF RICHARD SONN

Son of Mr. and Mrs. Ray Sonn

Mr. and Mrs. Sonn will take part in the Kiddush Service and will be host to the Congregation at the reception in honor of the Bar Mitzvah, following our services.

Co-Chairmen Kenneth Marks and Virginia Bobbin have announced plans for the Rally Dinner to be held December 2, Sunday evening.

You won't want to miss this one: Music, Dinner, Entertainment, and fun for all at the tiny price of 99¢.

SILVERPLATE will be an exciting affair this year -- with its Mexican theme. Get in on the ground floor, and COME TO THE FIESTA!

HELP WANTED !!

The Temple needs the advice and assistance of a professional Public Relations Counselor. If there is a member of our Congregation who has this qualification, and is willing to give his or her services, would he or she please call RO 4-4700 as soon as possible! The salary is nominal but the opportunities for advancement are great!

The Congregation mourns the death of our Past President, good friend, and loyal member:

HERMAN OSTROWSKY

We also mourn the death of our good friend and member of long standing:

JAMES KERNES

To both of their families, Temple Mizpah extends sincere sympathy.

ADULT STUDY GROUP TO DISCUSS CONFLICTS

The subjects for discussion in the Adult Education group for the coming weeks are the conflict between staunch followers of tradition, and those who challenged their positions. In the one instance, it was the controversy between the role of the Saducees and the new ideas of the Pharisees. In the other, it was the attempt to upset the basic traditional view of Jewish law, by a sect that insisted that only Torah was applicable and authoritative. The two conflicts are not parallel. The challengers won in the first struggle, but they lost in the second.

The subject for November 18, Pharisee vs. Saducee can help present-day Jews to understand the real mean-

(Continued on Page 2)

Temple Mizpah's newsletter was called the *Mizpah Forecast*. (Courtesy of Temple Judea Mizpah and Terry Kane.)

Congregation Anshe Lubavitch (men of Lubavitch), orthodox, was located at 7424 North Paullina Street. It moved to Rogers Park in 1954 when its Lawndale building was sold. Its rabbi was Solomon Hecht who had been their spiritual leader since 1942. They later moved to the Birchwood Nursing Home at 1426 West Birchwood Avenue. (Courtesy of Irving Cutler.)

The Rogers Park Jewish Community Center (JCC) was housed in an old home to answer the needs for a Jewish community center where its youth could play sports as well as other group activities. It helped foster a sense of community and kept the young people involved with other Jewish people. The center was open to all youth regardless of their faith. (Author's collection.)

The B'nai Jacob (children of Jacob) Congregation of Rogers Park (West Ridge) was built in 1952, while the congregation was established in 1944. It was located at 6200 North Artesian Avenue. In the 1990s, they merged with Skokie Valley Traditional. The building is currently used as a Hispanic church. Religious leaders who served this shul were Rabbi Joseph Gorfinkel, Rabbi Louis Sacks, and Rabbi Norman Lewison. (Courtesy of Irving Cutler.)

B'nai Jacob Hebrew School and Community Center is currently part of the local public school system. (Author's collection.)

This photograph shows the interior of the sanctuary of B'nai Jacob. (Author's collection.)

The stained-glass windows from B'nai Jacob were done in the Jewish tradition often honoring the memory of a departed loved one. Also known as "windows to heaven," the stained glass portrays scenes from the Bible. (Author's collection.)

The Beacon

OF THE
B'nai Jacob Congregation
of West Rogers Park

AFFILIATED WITH THE UNITED SYNAGOGUE OF AMERICA

SANCTUARY
BENJAMIN & ANNE KAPLAN HALL

DR. LOUIS L. SACKS, RABBI • MAX GORENSTEIN, PRESIDENT

CARL & BERTHA MILLER SCHOOL
BUILDING & COMMUNITY CENTER

CHANUKAH HOME SERVICE

Light first candle on Sunday, December 15th, after sunset.

The "Shammes" Candle(Servant candle) is not counted as a candle. It is only used in lighting the other candles. The individual candles are put in place starting with the righthand side of the Menorah. The Shammes is lit first.Then the candles are lighted from left to right, i.e. the last one placed in the Menorah is the first to be lit. The Hanukkah lights must burn at least half an hour each night. On Friday eve, the Hanukkah lights are kindled before Sabbath lights.

(The candles are kindled with the Shammes candle; one on the first evening, two on the second; until the eighth night of Hannukkah eight candles are lit. The following blessings are sung or recited.)
1. Boruch Atoh Adonoy, Elehenu Melech Hoolom, asher kidd'shonu, bmitsvosov, vtsivonu, l'hadlik ner shel'ch chanukah.
(Blessed are Thou, O Lord our God, Ruler of the Universe, Who has sanctified us by Thy commandments and commanded us to kindle the lights of Chanukah.)
2. Boruch Atoh Adonoy, Elohenu Melech hoolom, sheosoh nissim laavosenu, bavomin hohaim bazz'man hazreh.
(Blessed are Thou, O Lord our God, Ruler of the Universe, Who hast wrought miracles for our Fathers, in the days of old at this season.)

(Blessing recited on first night only)

Boruch Atoh Adonoy, Elohenu Melech hoolom Sheheck, yonu vkimonu, V'higgionu laz'man Hazreh.

Blessed Art Thou, O Lord our God, Ruler of the Universe, who has kept us in life and hast preserved us, and enables us to reach this season

Often the synagogue newsletter was the social register of the local congregational community. The newsletter of Congregation B'nai Jacob is seen here. (Courtesy of Rabbi Rallis Wiesenthal.)

Temple Beth El (house of God) is one of the oldest Jewish reform houses of worship in the city of Chicago, having been established in 1871. This structure is located at 3050 West Touhy Avenue and was built in 1957 for the congregation moving from their Palmer Square location. Their longest serving rabbi emeritus, Victor Weisberg, is still active at their Northbrook temple after more than 50 years at Beth El. (Courtesy of Temple Beth El and Vicki McKay.)

The cornerstone of Temple Beth El is seen here after being mortared into the main entrance in 1957. (Courtesy of Temple Beth El and Vicki McKay.)

A speech was given before groundbreaking ceremonies of Temple Beth El in 1956. (Courtesy of Temple Beth El and Vicki McKay.)

This is a rare photograph of the actual groundbreaking of the new Temple Beth El. (Courtesy of Temple Beth El and Vicki McKay.)

Temple Beth El

Confirmation　　　　　**Class of 1959**

Stanley Bach　Carole Blumenthal　Jordan Epstein　Gail Furer　Susan Gordon　Robin Heiss　Ilene Jacobs

Joan Kimmel

Steven Lewin

Susan Lewin　Steven Loevy　Rabbi Victor Weissberg　Arthur Marcus　Barbara Nester

Judith Rabin　Ricka Saleson　Barry Siegal　Marvin Siegal　Hilarie Simon　Joan Singer　Charles Stepner

Harry R. Hoyt Studio 2812 W. Devon, Chicago

The 1959 confirmation of Temple Beth El is seen here. (Courtesy of Temple Beth El and Vicki McKay.)

Rabbi Victor Weissberg and a class of recent bar mitzvah students are seen here in this 1960s photograph. (Courtesy of Temple Beth El and Vicki McKay.)

temple Beth-El of chicago

BULLETIN

VOL. 108 NUMBER 4   2 CHESHVAN 5738   OCTOBER 14, 1977

Sabbath Services

FRIDAY EVENING, OCT. 14th   **8:20 P.M.**

The Rabbis will conduct the Services and Preach Mr. and Mrs. Charles Rivkin will bless the lights, lead us in the Kiddush and host the Oneg Shabbat.

SATURDAY MORNING, OCT. 15th 10:45 A.M.

We will celebrate the Bar Mitzvah of

Tom Rivkin

Son of Mr. and Mrs. Charles Rivkin

SUNDAY EVENING, OCT. 16th   **7:30 P.M.**

Max Dimont will speak on:
"THE INDESTRUCTIBLE JEWS"

FRIDAY EVENING, OCT 21st

Dinner: 6:00 P.M.
Services: 8:20 P.M.

New Member Shabbat

The Rabbis will conduct the Services and Preach

SATURDAY MORNING, OCT. 22nd 10:45 A.M.

We will celebrate the Bar Mitzvah of

Michael Lerner

Son of Mr. and Mrs. Richard Lerner

Message from The Rabbi . . .

Many people believe that there should be a normal let down after such climatic moments as the High Holidays. This is not the Jewish concept. We begin the year on high and we continue by progressing still higher. To that end many of your fellow congregants have been working and planning and they now present a series of programs that are filled with meaning and enjoyment. This is so in our Religious School, at Services and in the full swept of our programming. People, your friends and neighbors express their dedication to knowledge, wisdom and understanding by their efforts. Those efforts are great in themselves. However, they are meant to be even more meaningful because they are an invitation to join them in opportunities for further growth and development. Please help us make this year a year of beauty and blessing, become more fully immersed in temple life and what it represents. If it does not meet your fullest needs, we stand ready to help you and help ourselves at the same time. We are open to ideas and welcome your help in making them meaningful for a larger community. Do not allow yourself merely to remain unnamed on a list. Be part of the vitality of Jewish life.

Rabbi

Sabbath Service Ushers

FRIDAY, OCT. 7th	FRIDAY, OCT. 14th
Arnold Weil, Capt.	Russel Morris, Capt.
Hy Nickow	Howard Steinman
Max Holtzman	Ralph Fine
Kalvin Kahn	Mel Silverbrandt

FRIDAY, OCT. 21st
Len Gaynon, Capt.
Ron Weissbuch
Jerome Katz
Roger Hirsch

Here is a copy of the newsletter of Temple Beth El from 1977. (Courtesy of Temple Beth El and Vicki McKay.)

The Conservative Jewish Congregation was built as the New Israel Congregation in 1960 and was later bought by Temple Ezra in 1966. Its membership is made up of survivors of the German Holocaust who established their temple in 1938. Rabbi Ira Sud, Rabbi Joseph Liberles, and cantor Moses Schwimmer led the congregation for decades. (Courtesy of Rabbi Rallis Wiesenthal.)

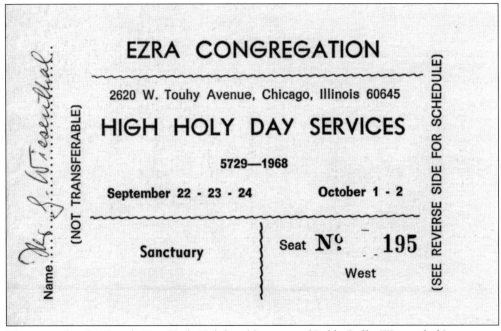

EZRA CONGREGATION

2620 W. Touhy Avenue, Chicago, Illinois 60645

HIGH HOLY DAY SERVICES

5729—1968

September 22 · 23 · 24   October 1 · 2

Sanctuary   Seat N⁰ 195

West

Name....

(NOT TRANSFERABLE)

(SEE REVERSE SIDE FOR SCHEDULE)

This is a ticket for Temple Ezra High Holiday. (Courtesy of Rabbi Rallis Wiesenthal.)

CONGREGATION EZRA-HABONIM NEWSLETTER

OCTOBER 1986

ELUL 5746-TISHRI 5747

IMPORTANT EVENTS IN OCTOBER

Oct. 1 Sisterhood Open Meeting
3 Eve of Rosh Hashanah
4 1st Day Rosh Hashanah
5 2nd Day Rosh Hashanah
8 Congregational Board Meeting
10 Family Service, 7 PM. Regular Service, 8:15 PM
12 Eve of Yom Kippur - Kol Nidre
13 Yom Kippur
15 Men's Club & Sisterhood Boards
17 Eve of Sukkot
18 1st Day Sukkot
19 2nd Day Sukkot
24 Hoshana Rabba
25 Shmini Atzeret - YIZKOR
26 Simchat Torah

COMING EVENTS

Nov. 2 Sisterhood Membership Luncheon
Adult Education begins
9 Krystallnacht Service, 7 PM
14 Family Service, 7 PM
16 Men's Club Breakfast, with Adult Education
22)
23) Rummage Sale
30 Sisterhood Supper Party

VIEWPOINT

COMING BACK

Annabel and I had many fascinating experiences this past summer during a tour of mainland China. You will hear about some of our adventures during the High Holy Days. There was one site we visited, however, that continues to boggle my mind.

There is a magnificent Pagoda in Bejing (Peking), called the Temple of Heavenly Peace. It is very ornate and very old. The Pagoda was used only by the Emperor. It was used only one day a year. The Emperor would enter the Pagoda and spend a 24 hour period fasting, engaging in self-criticism, and praying for the welfare of the people.

The parallel between the actions of the Emperor and the ritual of the High Priest in the Holy of Holies on the Temple Mount during Yom Kippur indeed left me wide-eyed. For our purposes, it is not important to know which religion developed this idea first, although I will attempt to find out whether there has been any scholarly research done on this remarkable parallel. Rather, the similarity of religious expression suggests a spiritual spark, which I am convinced is inherent in each human being.

Many people characterize themselves as not being "religious." They do so because they measure themselves solely on the basis of ritual observance, and neglect to see our tradition and their being religious in terms of compassion, morality, justice or loving-kindness. Such people err, and deny themselves the spiritual growth they are capable of achieving. In denying their spirituality, such people can never make room for adopting the ritual actions which enhance and affirm their spiritual core. To be a Jew means to incorporate both the ethical-spiritual and the ritual teachings of our faith.

We all recognize that one can be a very decent person-Jew without even stepping foot into a Synagogue or lighting Shabbat candles. One can also be punctilious in ritual observances and still be morally bankrupt.

The point is that such onesidedness is really not a fruitful option. We need both. And if we are deficient, then we need to work harder to perfect our lives.

(Continued Page 2)

The newsletter of Congregation Ezra-Habonim is seen here. (Courtesy of Rabbi Rallis Wiesenthal.)

Congregation Ezra-Habonim (builders) was the result of a merger in 1973 of the North Side Temple Ezra (1938) and the South Shore Congregation Habonim (1950s), which both share the distinction of having among their original members survivors of Adolf Hitler's Germany. (Courtesy of Rabbi Rallis Wiesenthal.)

This High Holiday ticket shows the new merger of Temple Ezra with Congregation Habonim to form Congregation Ezra-Habonim. (Courtesy of Rabbi Rallis Wiesenthal.)

For the 50th anniversary of Kristallnacht (night of broken glass) a booklet was issued describing of the beginning of the Holocaust. (Courtesy of Rabbi Rallis Wiesenthal.)

North town Congregation Ner Tamid (eternal light) was erected in 1938 at West Rosemont and North California Avenues as a conservative Jewish synagogue. It later merged with Ezra-Habonim in the 1980s. Its spiritual leaders were Rabbi Benjamin Birnbaum and Rabbi Samuel Klein. After nearly 70 years, the membership has voted to put the buildings up for sale in 2007. They are contemplating a merger with another Egalitarian Conservative group. (Author's collection.)

Note the beautiful stained-glass windows and elegant wood interiors in the Ner Tamid sanctuary. (Author's collection.)

January 1, 1973   Vol. 10 No. 4   27 Tevet 5733

FROM OUR CONGREGATION PRESIDENT

The search for a successor to Rabbi Stanley J. Schachter is going forward under the direction of a large committee headed by Vice-President, Albert H. Wittlin, Ritual Chairman.

No avenue is being overlooked so that our Congregation will continue to have the kind of leadership we have enjoyed these many years.

For the immediate future, it is less likely that such a selection will be made, as most Rabbis have contracts terminating at the High Holidays.

Be assured, we will have interim guest Rabbis officiating at Sabbath and Holiday services, and these Rabbis will be available to our members for Rabbinical services as needed.

MAYER WEINSHANK

GUEST RABBIS

We are pleased to announce that Rabbi Naphtali Rubinger, of Habonim Congregation will be our guest Rabbi on:

January 5 & 6, 1973
January 12 & 13, 1973

Rabbi David Graubart will be our guest Rabbi on
January 19 & 20, 1973
January 26 & 27, 1973

We thank Rabbi Burton Cohen, Director of Camp Ramah, for being with us in December. It always is a pleasure to have Rabbi Cohen with us as a worshipper as well as in the pulpit.   RITUAL COMMITTEE

KINDLE SABBATH LIGHTS

Friday, January 5, 1973, 4:23 P.M.
Friday, January 12, 1973, 4:30 P.M.
Friday, January 19, 1973, 4:38 P.M.
Friday, January 26, 1973, 4:46 P.M.
Friday evening services in
Beth Hamedresh

SABBATH WORSHIP

SATURDAY, JANUARY 13, 1973, 8:45 A.M.
JOSE MACHABANSKI
Son of MR. & MRS. LEO MACHABANSKI will be called to the Torah as a Bar Mitzvah

SATURDAY, JANUARY 27, 1973, 8:45 A.M.
DAVID BAER
Son of MR. & MRS. RUBIN BAER will be called to the Torah as a Bar Mitzvah

FRIDAY, JANUARY 12, 1973, 8:30 P.M.
SISTERHOOD SABBATH

FRIDAY EVENING SERVICES 8:30 P.M.

SATURDAY MORNING SERVICES 8:45 A.M.
in the Sanctuary

CANTOR DAVID BRANDHANDLER WILL OFFICIATE AT THESE SERVICES. THE SYNAGOGUE CHOIR DIRECTED BY DAVID MINKUS SINGS AT FRIDAY EVENING SERVICES.

ADULT EDUCATION SERIES "JEWISH MYSTICISM"

The Adult Education Series this year will open on Wednesday, January 24, 1973, at 8 P.M. and continue on alternate Wednesdays through April 4th.

Outstanding Jewish scholars, who have been acclaimed for their original work in the field of Jewish Mysticism, will head the individual programs, which this year will be presented by B'nai Zion, Shaare Tikvah and Ner Tamid Congregations, acting as the Joint Adult Education Council.

The series will be rotated among the three synagogues. Three Chicago Rabbis: Dr. Monford Harris, Dr. Byron Sherwin and Dr. Samuel H. Dresner; and Dr. Seymour Siegel of the Jewish Theological Seminary, will be the lecturers for the series (two by Dr. Harris). The last of the series will be a musical extravaganza headed by Neil Levin, M.A., of Columbia University, who will have the Cantors of the three sponsoring Congregations and an augmented choir to present traditional Jewish music.

The cost of the complete series will be $10.00 per person. A brochure with all the details will be in the mail.

This Ner Tamid newsletter lists a rabbi. It has become increasingly difficult to find full-time rabbis given the budgetary constraints of many congregations. (Courtesy of Congregation Ner Tamid-Ezra Habonim.)

Congregation B'nai David moved its synagogue in the early 1950s to the Budlong Woods community after being a fixture for nearly 50 years in the Humboldt Park neighborhood. As seen in this recent photograph, it has changed function to become a Korean temple.

Mikro Kodish Anshe Ticktin (holy scripture, men of Ticktin) the Ravenswood/Budlong synagogue was the result of a merger of Atereth Israel Anshe Ticktin and Mikro Kodish Lida and Pinsk. These Lawndale shuls made the necessary move northward as the old West Side went through its dynamic change in the 1950s. Its religious leader was Rabbi Albert H. Ellison. In 2004, the shrinking congregation changed and made the move to a Lubuvacher congregation reflecting their changing neighborhood. (Author's collection.)

The Home of the Association of the Jewish Blind, located at 3525 West Foster Avenue, was one of the many communal organizations designed to take care of the infirmed within the Jewish community. The successor of the West Side organization, the home was active in the Budlong community for over 50 years. (Author's collection.)

The cornerstone of the Association of the Jewish Blind is pictured here. (Author's collection.)

Located at 4920 North Kimball Avenue, Congregation Beth Jacob (house of Jacob) was the leading traditional synagogue in the Albany Park/Hollywood Park neighborhood. Their long-serving spiritual leader was Rabbi Haskell Lehrfield. After struggling with the changing community, seeing all the younger families move further north in the city or to the suburbs, the membership elected to sell their building. (Courtesy of Irving Cutler.)

The ever-changing demographics of the Albany Park community are seen here. Congregation Beth Jacob sold their building to the Korean Assembly of God. (Courtesy of Irving Cutler.)

The oldest orthodox congregation in the Albany Park area, Beth Itzchock (house of Isaac), was established in 1919. The synagogue was erected in 1922 and was located at 4645 North Drake Avenue. Rabbi Isaac Siegel and Rabbi Aaron Rine were the long-serving religious leaders for most of its first 50 years. (Courtesy of Irving Cutler.)

Since many orthodox congregations did not have a choir, the cantor was the spiritual music center of the sanctuary; the rare exception was Beth Itzchock. Seen here is the renowned cantor Tevele Cohen with choir.

THE VOICE of BETH ITZCHOK of ALBANY PARK

"The House Where the Ideals of Isaac are Perpetuated:

CONG. BETH ITZCHOK
4645 N. Drake Ave.
Chicago 25, Ill.
IRving 8-6416

AARON M. RINE, RABBI   D. TEVELE COHEN, CANTOR

VOL. II   OCTOBER 1951 -- TISHRE 5712   NO. 2.

תקע בשופר גדול

לשנה טובה תכתבו
"Be inscribed for a good year!"

ROSH HASHANAH -- 5712

BLOW THE GREAT HORN
FOR OUR LIBERATION

ON ROSH HASHANAH THEY
ARE INSCRIBED

The Jewish New Year (Rosh Hashonah) 5712 will be ushered in with sunset Sunday, September 30, and will extend through nightfall Tuesday, October 2. This holiday is also called "Yom Hazikoron", the Day of Remembrance, for on this day all acts of Man and nations are reviewed by the Almighty and judged for the coming year. It is also designated in the Bible As "Yom Truah," the day for the sounding of the Shofar (ram's horn.)

The awe-inspiring and soul-stiring sounds of the Shofar are sounded several times in the course of the service. First it is sounded before the "Musaf", then thrice during the "Musaf" liturgy, and again near the conclusion of the service. The SHOFAR calls every worshipper to reflect on his past deeds, and to resolve to improve them.

In the main Synagogue auditorium, Cantor D. Tevele Cohen and choir will chant the services, Rabbi Aaron M. Rine will render English readings and explanations and will deliver the sermons. Adler's Hebrew-English prayer books will be used.

Services in our Social Center will be conducted by Student-Rabbi Milton H. Polin and will be chanted by Cantor Hyman Baim. The Beth Medrosh services will be chanted by Messrs. Louis Rosner and I. Elkin.

The schedule for Rosh Hashonah services is as follows: Sunday evening, 5:15 P.M.; Mon. & Tues. mornings 7:00 A.M. (at Center 8:00 A.M.)

At 3 P.M. Monday, children of the Beth Itzchok Hebrew and Sunday Schools will walk to the creek on Drake past Argyle, for the traditional "Tashlich" service.

A special service for young-adults will be held Monday afternoon, 4:00 o'clock at the Center to be conducted by Rabbi Polin. Evening (Micha) service, 5:00 P.M. to be followed by a Yiddish address by Rabbi Rine. Ma'ariv service, 6:P.M. There is no charge for this. Hebrew-English books and skull caps will be provided.

The period between Rosh Hashonah and Yom Kippur is known as "Aseres Y'may Teshuvoh," Ten Days of Panitence, at which time special prayers are inserted in the daily services.

"EVERYONE'S SIGNATURE
APPEARS THEREON"
(THE BOOK OF LIFE)

A TASHLICH SERVICE

A newsletter of Congregation Beth Itzchock from 1951 is pictured here. (Courtesy of Malke Rine Baskt.)

40

Rabbi Aaron Rine (right), the longest-serving religious leader of Beth Itzchock, is seen here with the president of the congregation and a board member at the start of the campaign for the Combined Jewish Appeal, the forerunner of the Jewish United Fund. (Courtesy of Malke Rine Baskt.)

Seen here are Rabbi Aaron Rine and members of the board during the shofar ceremony of the Jewish new year, Rosh Hashanah, in the last days in their Albany Park location. (Courtesy of Malke Rine Baskt.)

Due to the refusal of the board of directors to sell the Beth Itzchock building, the building was allowed to decay. It was later torn down and the land donated by the City of Chicago for a community park. Here the facade can be seen just before the wrecking ball takes it down. (Courtesy of Norman D. Schwartz.)

Albany Park Hebrew Congregation, the North Lawndale Avenue shul, was the largest conservative congregation in Albany Park. Built in 1923 at 4601 North Lawndale Avenue, Albany Park Hebrew Congregation served the growing younger progressive Jewish population, and its beloved spiritual leader was Rabbi Abraham E. Abramowitz and later Rabbi Ephraim Prombaum. This photograph was taken after the building was sold. (Courtesy of Norman D. Schwartz.)

This photograph is of the 1951 Albany Park Hebrew Congregation graduating confirmation class. (Courtesy of June Sochen.)

Temple Beth Israel (house of Israel) was the first temple and the only reform congregation in Albany Park. Established in 1917, the building was constructed in 1922 at 4850 North Bernard Avenue. Rabbi Felix Mendelsohn was its first spiritual leader, later followed by the long-serving Rabbi Ernst Lorge. This photograph is of the original architectural rendering by the architectural firm of Halperin and Braun. Due to the high cost of this design, another less-costly design was chosen by the board of directors. (Courtesy of Temple Beth Israel.)

A simpler, more modern-looking design is depicted here in this 1923 rendering from Hyman L. Meites's *History of the Jews of Chicago.*

This is the final rendering of the winning modern design of Temple Beth Israel from 1922. (Courtesy of Temple Beth Israel.)

By the late 1970s, the demographics of Albany Park had changed significantly, warranting one of the last remaining congregations to relocate. Beth Israel is seen here shortly after it was converted into a Korean church. Later this same building was converted into a Pentecostal Romanian church. (Courtesy of Irving Cutler.)

This is Temple Beth Israel around 1940. Shown is the celebration of simcah torah. (Courtesy of Temple Beth Israel.)

HEBREW INSTITUTE OF ALBANY PARK

"Center of Jewish Life and Activity"

4858 North Lawndale Avenue

EXTENDS CONGRATULATIONS AND BEST WISHES TO THE

Hebrew Theological College

of Chicago

In 1940, the Albany Park community had grown enough to merit its own Hebrew institution of higher learning. Here is the Hebrew Institute of Albany Park in the only rendering know to exist. It later became congregation Kehilath Jeshurun Synagogue. This photograph is from the 20th anniversary book of the Hebrew Theological College from 1942. (Courtesy of Charlotte Kaplan.)

Kehilath Jeshurun Synagogue (Congregation Jeshurun), located at 3703 West Ainslie Street, was the first of two Jewish congregations established as a conservative-only organization in Albany Park. The long-serving religious leader was Rabbi Abromovitz, and later Rabbi Prombaum and Rabbi Nathan Levinson. (Courtesy of Irving Cutler.)

Of the many traditional shuls in the Albany Park community, Congregation Mount Sinai at 4332 North Kedzie Avenue had a small but dedicated following. Its rabbi was Adam Neuberger. (Courtesy of Irving Cutler.)

Congregation Oir Israel (light of Israel) was located at 4610 North Kedzie Avenue and was a well-established orthodox synagogue in the Albany Park neighborhood. Their spiritual leaders were Rabbi H. Schaffer and Rabbi David M. Lieberman. This photograph, taken in 1977, shows the population changing from Jewish and Korean to immigrants of Middle Eastern nationality. (Courtesy of Irving Cutler.)

Of great importance to all communities, the Jewish communal buildings were gathering places for social issues. They dealt with common everyday concerns such as preschool, nursery school, as well regular religious day school. Seen here is the Arie Crown Hebrew Day School, which was later relocated to Skokie. (Courtesy of Irving Cutler.)

Of the many social organizations supported by the Albany Park Jewish community, the Deborah Boys Club was the epicenter of the neighborhood, located at North Kimball Avenue and West Argyle Street. Here boys of all ages would polish there athletic skills on the basketball court. Many sports and other activities were available to the Jewish youth of the area. (Courtesy of Irving Cutler.)

The first prototype of the modern Jewish community center was the Max Straus Jewish Community Center, which was established in Albany Park in 1941. It was located at 3715 West Wilson Avenue. (Courtesy of the Jewish Community Center and Chicago Historical Society.)

A group of pre-scholars poses at the Max Straus Jewish Community Center in 1954. (Courtesy of the Jewish Community Center and Chicago Historical Society.)

Community playhouse and theatrical productions were a mainstay at the Max Straus Jewish Community Center, as seen in this advertisement from the 1940s. (Courtesy of the Jewish Community Center.)

Not all synagogues were based on formal Jewish ritual. Seen here is a group based on Zionist principals, located at West Foster and North Kimball Avenues. Hapoal Hamizrachi (religious socialist Zionists) was such a group. (Courtesy of Irving Cutler.)

The Ark located on Lawrence Avenue was the center of retail fund-raising for the community. The store would take in donated clothing, furniture, art, and other items to sell and raise money for the Jewish community. (Courtesy of Irving Cutler.)

The largest conservative congregation in Logan Square was Logan Square Congregation/Shaare Zedek (gates of righteousness). Established in 1916, it was located at 3125 West Fullerton Avenue. The building sanctuary was dedicated in 1922, and the first rabbi was Aaron Cohen. Later prominent rabbis were Benjamin Birnbaun, Emanuel Bennett, and Lawrence Charney. (Courtesy of the Steve Grubman 1976 Collection.)

This photograph of the synagogue interior is of the synagogue founding pioneers of Logan Square/Shaare Zedek and shows a marble tablet from 1922 that lists the past and current officers. (Courtesy of Judge Jerry Orbach.)

This rare rendering is from a promotional piece created for Temple Beth El's 1940s membership drive. (Courtesy of Temple Beth El and Vicki McKay.)

The 1923 confirmation class of Beth El was the first since moving to the Palmer Square location. The class is seen here with Rabbi Gusfield. (Courtesy of Temple Beth El and Vicki McKay.)

Since there are no known photographs available of Temple Beth El, these contemporary photographs show the classic lines of this 1923 building. It was located at 3220 West Palmer Street. Although it has been a Chicago Boys Club for nearly 50 years, its motto, Knowledge, Service and Truth, can still be seen. (Author's collection.)

Temple Beth El's Hebrew school also served as its social and community center. As in many neighborhoods where the Jewish population was not the predominant group, this community center often served the entire area sponsoring youth baseball and other activities. (Author's collection.)

As is often the case in Jewish communities, there is but one reform temple, Beth El (house of God) is one of the oldest un-reconstituted congregations in the Chicago metropolitan area, having been established in Chicago since 1871. The beloved, revered Rabbi Paul Goren, who was also one of the leading U.S. Army chaplains during World War II, served the temple from 1939 to 1949. (Courtesy of Temple Beth El and Vicki McKay.)

WEEKLY  BULLETIN

BETH-EL JEWISH CONGREGATION
A MEMBER OF THE UNION OF AMERICAN HEBREW CONGREGATIONS

3230 Palmer Street | Rabbi Paul Gorin, Chaplain H. S. A. / JOSEPH M. STRAUSS, Acting Rabbi | Belmont 6001

Friday March 8th

RABBI JOSEPH M. STRAUSS

WILL TALK ON

A REPORT ON THE UNION BIENNIAL

Our Social Hour hostesses this Friday evening will be Mrs. William Reiger, Mrs. George Reiger and Mrs. H. Burton Schatz.

* * * * * * * * * * * * * * * * *

CHAPLAIN GORIN SOLEMNIZES FIRST D.P. WEDDING

Minchen, Germany: "The Jewish Chaplain, Paul Gorin from Chicago, had the honor to solemnize the first Jewish Displaced Persons wedding in Bad Taltz, the chief sector of the Third Army. The entire Jewish community, consisting of forty-seven people who were delivered from the hand of the Nazis by the Third Army, attended the ceremony.

"Chaplain Gorin performed the wedding with deep emotion and said that 'this wedding symbolizes the new life to come for the Jewish people'.

"The refreshments that followed the ceremony were furnished by Cpl. Herbert Pflauster of New York City, who likewise cooked Gefilte Fish and brought Kosher salami which had been sent him by his relatives in New York. The room was decorated with blue and white flags inscribed with the slogan "Am Yisroel Chai" ... (Israel Lives Eternal).

* * * * * * * * * * * * * * * * *

SISTERHOOD MEETING MARCH 12TH

The monthly Sisterhood Meeting will be devoted to a report of the decisions reached at the Sisterhood Convention last week.

The meeting will convene at 1:30 P.M. Refreshments will be served.

* * * * * * * * * * * * * * * * *

RABBINICAL "KALLAH"

The annual meeting of the Chicago Rabbinical Association known as "Kallah" will be held on the afternoon and evening of March 10th at the College of Jewish Studies, 72 E. 11th St.

The afternoon session will be addressed by Professor William F. Albright, of Johns Hopkins University. He will discuss "MONOTHEISM AND PAGANISM IN EARLY ISRAEL". The other subject for discussion will be "THE RESPONSIBILITY OF THE RABBINATE TO RETURNING VETERANS" by Chaplains Morton Berman and Charles Shulman.

The evening session will be dedicated to the fortieth anniversary of the literary labors of Dr. Meyer Waxman, author of "The History of Jewish Literature" and will be featured by a special musical program rendered by Cantor Moses Silverman and the Halevi Choral Society.

PURIM CARNIVAL
BY BETH-EL RELIGIOUS SCHOOL AT TEMPLE SUN. AFTERNOON MARCH 17th AT 2:30 PM
GAMES-PLAYS-SONGS-REFRESHMENTS
ADMISSION--35¢

This weekly news bulletin from 1943 tells of the upcoming Purim festival. Notice the name of the acting rabbi, Joseph Strauss, who was later to become the longest serving rabbi of Temple Menorah in West Rogers Park. Newsletters and bulletins were often the most efficient way to communicate in an era of few telephones. (Courtesy of Temple Beth El and Vicki McKay.)

The first home for aged Jews was established in 1942 in the Palmer Square neighborhood. State senator, and later judge, Michael Zlatnik was the prime mover in creating this communal home for the aging population. The Northwest Home for the Aged is a series of buildings originally built by a sea captain for his daughters. (Author's collection.)

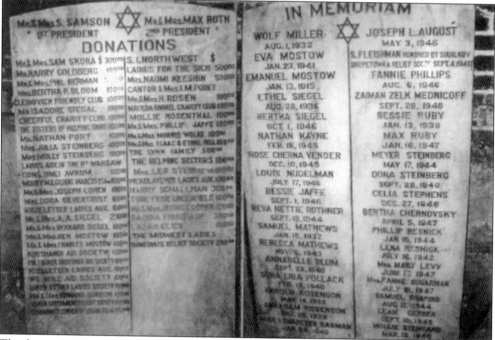

The former Northwest Home for the Aged is now a condominium. During a recent inspection of the buildings basement and structure by Steve Kroeckel, he uncovered the original donation in memorial marble tablets. (Author's collection.)

Two

NORTHWEST SIDE

The first synagogue built in Humboldt Park was the Austrian Galician shul in 1911. Known for its orthodoxy and adherence to ritual, it did not have a choir. What they lacked in a choir was made up with a talented cantor, Metropolitan Opera company star Richard Tucker. His chanting (singing) of the High Holiday prayers was the religious equivalent of going to an operatic concert. He was often seen sitting on a bench during a break in the Yom Kippur services practicing his cantorial rhythms. Other famous cantors were Todros Greenberg and Yossele Rosenblatt. Their long-serving religious leader was Rabbi Moses Eichenstein. The synagogue closed in 1957, when they merged with Beth Israel of Peterson Park to become A. G. Beth Israel. (Author's collection.)

Congregation Atereth Zion (crown of Zion), a traditional congregation known as the Spaulding Avenue shul, was located at 1132 North Spaulding Avenue on the west side of Humboldt Park and was built in 1920. Their religious leaders were Rabbi Marbodetsky, Rabbi Finke, and Rabbi Gordon. Their last cantor was the renowned Anchell Friedman. They closed their doors in the mid-1960s. (Author's collection.)

This magnificent synagogue was classically designed with some of the most beautiful stained-glass windows created. Still visible from the ceiling in the interior of the main sanctuary is this Star of David window. (Author's collection.)

The North Humboldt Boulevard shul, B'nai David/Ohave Zedek (children of David/lovers of righteousness) quickly adapted to the progressive conservative Jewish philosophy. Erected in 1919 and located at 1910 North Humboldt Boulevard, this congregation traces its roots to the Division Street neighborhood with its founding in 1905. Its early religious leaders were Rabbis Israel Elfenbein and Dr. Joseph Hevesh. It straddled the Logan Square and Humboldt Park neighborhoods and was a very popular synagogue with the younger members of the community. Its later rabbis were Louis Sacks and Benjamin Birnbaum. It later relocated to the North Park/Budlong Woods neighborhood at 2626 West Foster Avenue. (Author's collection.)

The lintel of the North Humboldt Boulevard shul is seen here. (Author's collection.)

The Haddon Avenue shul, B'nai Yakov (children of Jacob), was a popular orthodox synagogue on the Northwest Side located at 2700 West Haddon Avenue, a few blocks east of Humboldt Park. It was built just after World War I. Its religious leaders were Rabbi Peretz Dissen and Rabbi Chaim Yudkowsky. It closed in 1975, and the building was sold in 1979. (Author's collection.)

This photograph was taken from the north side of B'nai Yakov and shows the old Star of David framing. The stained-glass window is now long gone from neglect. (Author's collection.)

This photograph of the stone lintel of B'nai Yakov is faded after nearly 90 years, but the Hebrew script is still quite visible. (Author's collection.)

Congregation Zemach Zedek (offspring of righteousness) was located at 1459 North Talman Avenue in the Division Street community on the Northwest Side. Its beloved long-serving spiritual leader was Rabbi Abraham Isaac Pearlstein. The congregation membership purchased this 1892 Lutheran church in the 1920s, and it closed in 1966. (Author's collection.)

The Hebrew name of Zemach Zedek is still visible on the stone lintel above the doorway after 80 years. (Author's collection.)

Congregation Tiperith Zion (the glory of Zion) was located at 1243 North Wolcott Avenue and was built in 1904 as one of the first orthodox synagogues on the Northwest Side. Rabbi S. H. Glick and Rabbi I. L. Gordon served the congregation for most of its early history. (Courtesy of Irving Cutler.)

Congregation Ezras Israel (aid of Israel) was located at 1300 North Artesian Avenue and was the leading orthodox, later traditional, synagogue on the old Northwest Side. It was established in 1904 in a small frame home on Shober Street. The members purchased a Protestant church in 1920 and converted it into a synagogue. For the next 50 years, Ezras Israel was led by two spiritual giants of their age, Rabbi Hirsch Mayer Rosenblum, known as the "Red Rabbi" for his red beard not his politics, and the beloved Rabbi Israel Miller. (Courtesy of Irving Cutler.)

In its second move, this time to the Northwest Side in 1902, Temple Beth El built this traditional structure to meet the demands of its ever-increasing membership, coupled with the desire to be located in the popular Northwest Side. It was located at 2126 West Crystal Street. Its rabbi for over 20 years was the venerable Dr. Julius Rappaport. Other important rabbis were Julian Gusfield and Mayer Lipman. (Courtesy of *History of the Jews of Chicago*.)

Beth El's Molner Community Center, built in 1902, is today a condominium. (Author's collection.)

Congregation Beth Hillel U' Nachalath Mosheh (house of Hillel the inheritors of Moses) was established in the 1930s on the farthest portion of the Northwest Side. It was located at 3845 North Lamon Avenue. Although the congregation and building no longer exist, they represented a small but strong congregation of men and women in area not known for having many Jewish people in their community, near West Diversey and North Central Avenues. Their spiritual leaders were Abraham Lapin and Rabbi Solomon Schottland. It was torn down in the 1960s; there are no known photographs. (Courtesy of Allen Sered.)

ANNUAL YEAR BOOK

Congregation
Beth Hillel U'Nachalath Mosheh
and
Women's Auxiliary
3845 North Lamon Avenue, Chicago, Ill

Tenth
ANNUAL FUND RAISING DINNER
DECEMBER 14th, 1947
TEL AVIV RESTAURANT
CHICAGO, ILLINOIS

We join our Brethren throughout the universe in expressing our deep gratitude to the United Nations General Assembly for their vote to partition the Holy Land into Jewish and Arab States beginning next October 1st.

May our Arab neighbors quickly see the light, so that we can dwell forever together in peace and harmony.

The inscription on the back of the anniversary booklet shows the optimism that was never realized, and to this day the promise of peace is ever allusive. (Courtesy of Allen Sered.)

Herzl Community Home was the main social center of the Humboldt Park Jewish community. Built in 1926 on North California Avenue across from the park, Herzl held dances and workshops for new immigrants, as well as fiery Socialist meetings. (Author's collection.)

As is often the case, it is sometimes impossible to ascertain what type of building one is looking at. During a recent rainstorm, the past was revealed and the name of the Herzl Community Home once again became visible, if only for a brief moment. (Author's collection.)

Three

CITY CENTRAL

Congregation Anshe Emes (men of truth), later Anshe Mizrachi (men of the east), was located at 627 West Patterson Avenue, formerly Gary Place, in the Lakeview neighborhood and was built in 1922 from their location on North Sedgwick Street. It was an early member of the Jewish conservative movement. Its early religious leader was Rabbi Phillip A. Langh. This image is from the Anshe Emet 100th anniversary book. (Courtesy of Bob Krakowsky.)

The confirmation class of 1941 poses in this photograph. (Courtesy of Temple Emanuel.)

This is the class photograph of the confirmation class of 1940. (Courtesy of Temple Emanuel.)

Temple Emanuel was the first reform temple in the North Side Lakeview community located at 701 West Buckingham Place. It was built in 1907; it burned and was rebuilt in 1917. Rabbi Felix Levy and Rabbi Herman Schaalman led the congregation for most of its first 75 years. (Courtesy of *History of the Jews of Chicago*.)

The cornerstone and foundation wall of Temple Emanuel both survived the fire of 1917 and are still visible after 100 years. (Author's collection.)

Temple Ezra was established in 1936 as the North Center Youth Center. It changed its name to Temple Ezra in 1946 and adopted the conservative Jewish tradition. It moved to 836 West Aldine Avenue. This photograph was taken around 1948. Rabbi David Schoenbeger was the first full-time spiritual leader serving from 1946 to 1956, and he was succeeded by Rabbi Joseph Liberles. (Author's collection.)

Temple Ezra members often had their High Holiday service at Dr. Preston Bradley's Peoples Temple, which had more room for the congregation. (Courtesy of Rabbi Rallis Wiesenthal.)

Anshe Emet was founded in 1878, and after nearly 20 years, they were finally able to realize their dream of a synagogue of their own in 1893 at 1363 North Sedgwick Street. (Courtesy of Congregation Anshe Emet and Robert Krawkowsky.)

After moving to the Lakeview neighborhood in 1922, Congregation Anshe Emet sold their synagogue to Congregation B'nai Israel, who later merged with Lakeview Anshe Sholom and sold it to the Muslim Holy Temple of Islam. (Courtesy of Irving Cutler.)

North Chicago Hebrew Congregation (later Temple Sholom) came into existence in 1867. After years occupying many other buildings, the members decided to purchase lots at the corner at North LaSalle Street and West Goethe Street and erected their magnificent temple in 1892, which was dedicated in 1893. The early rabbis were Dr. A. Norden and Dr. A. Hirschberg. (Courtesy of Irving Cutler.).

Designed by the noted architect Alfred Alschuler in 1910, the new North Chicago Hebrew Congregation, now Temple Sholom, was dedicated in 1911 at Pine Grove and Grace. Note that the biblical quote above the lintel, "Mine House Shall Be Called an House of Prayer For All Peoples," is still visible. (Author's collection.)

ON THIS SITE STOOD,
IN 1851, THE FIRST JEWISH
HOUSE OF WORSHIP
IN THE STATE OF ILLINOIS
• • • • •

DEDICATED BY THE
JEWISH HISTORICAL SOCIETY
OF ILLINOIS OCT. 9. 1918

This plaque from 1918, dedicated by the Chicago Historical Society, shows the original site of the first Jewish house of worship, Kehilath Anshe Maariv (congregation men of the west), as being the Main Chicago Post Office. The congregation was formed in 1847. (Courtesy of *History of the Jews of Chicago.*)

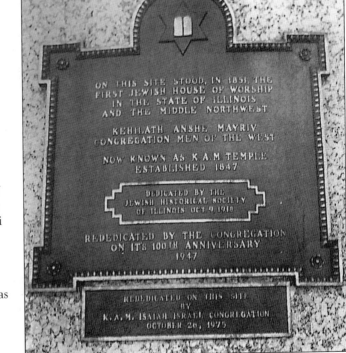

Following the demolition of the old Chicago Post Office in 1974, the new Klyucynski Federal Building was erected and dedicated in 1975 at which time a new plaque honoring the first Jewish House of Worship was also dedicated by Kehilath Anshe Maariv (KAM) Isaiah Israel Congregation. (Author's collection.)

Rabbi Isaac Chronic was the second spiritual leader of Chicago Sinai Congregation. He led the temple from 1864 to 1869. (Courtesy of Chicago Sinai Congregation.)

Chicago Sinai Congregation is the oldest un-reconstituted Jewish temple in the city of Chicago. Their first building was the former Trinity Episcopal Church originally located on West Madison Avenue and then later moved to West Monroe Street in 1861, just east of present-day North LaSalle Street. (Courtesy of the Central Trust Company of Illinois.)

Four

NEAR WEST SIDE

The Maxwell Street neighborhood had over 40 synagogues and communal buildings during its heyday. This Congregation Ahavas Achim (brotherhood of love), located 1251 South Newberry Street, was built around 1901. It later moved in the 1930s to the Northwest Side at 1228 North Claremont Avenue. It later merged with Beth Sholom on Jersey Avenue to become Beth Sholom Ahavas Achim and continues today at its present location of 5655 North Jersey Avenue. (Courtesy of the Charles W. Cushing Collection, Indiana University.)

Congregation Ohave Sholom (lovers of peace), later Anshe Sholom (men of peace), was located at the corner of West Polk Street and South Ashland Avenue at the outskirts of the Near West Side. Its early spiritual leader was Rabbi Glick, and later Rabbi Saul Silber. The building was erected in 1910 and designed by Alexander Levy. (Courtesy of the Chicago Historical Society.)

Zion Temple was the first temple designed by the renowned team of Dankmar Adler and Louis Sullivan in 1885 and was located at North Ogden Avenue and West Washington Boulevard. Zion was established as members of Isaiah Temple moved to the new West Side and were in need of their own house of worship. They later merged with B'nai Abraham and moved to the Garfield Park community on Washington Boulevard. (Courtesy of the Chicago Historical Society.)

B'nai Jehoshua (children of Jehoshua), a reform congregation, was established by a group of Bohemian Jewish businessmen who found a need for a temple of their own tradition. It was built in 1892 and was located at West Twentieth Street and South Ashland Avenue. (Courtesy of Congregation B'nai Jehoshua Beth Elohim.)

After moving north to Glenview and merging with Congregation Beth Elohim, the membership sold their old building to St. Pius Catholic Church. It was later torn down. (Courtesy of Irving Cutler.)

The Service Club of the Chicago Hebrew Institute was one of the many clubs and groups that offered programs from Red Cross training to the Golden Agers. (Courtesy of the Jewish Community Centers of Chicago.)

This 1920 photograph shows that education was of equal importance to the board as were the sports activates. Here the graduating class of the newly minted (former greenhorns) citizens to be can be seen. (Courtesy of the Jewish Community Centers of Chicago.)

Five

WEST SIDE

Beth Hamidrash Hagadol (great house of study), located at West Douglas Boulevard and South St. Louis Avenue, was built in 1916. It was the result of the splitting of the West Maxwell Street synagogue of the same name whose members elected to divide the proceeds from the sale of their synagogue and build two separate congregations, one for the new West Side and one for their South Side members at 5129 South Indiana Avenue. (Courtesy of *History of the Jews of Chicago*.)

Kehilath Jacob was located at the juncture of Douglas Boulevard and Independence Boulevard. It was built in 1915. The spiritual leader was Rabbi Joseph Kagan. After dominance as one of the largest orthodox synagogues with a large independent Hebrew school, the membership voted to relocate to the Far North Side community of Hollywood/Petersen Park where they merged with Congregation Beth Samuel in the 1950s. (Courtesy of *History of the Jews of Chicago*.)

Kanesseth Israel Nusach S'fard, Assembly of Israel Sephardic Tradition (KINS) was located at 1308 South Independence Boulevard and was built in 1921. One of the last religious leaders was Rabbi Aaron Rine, who later became the long-serving rabbi of Beth Itchock of Albany Park. (Courtesy of *History of the Jews of Chicago*.)

Congregation Anshe Sholom (men of peace) was located at South Independence Boulevard and West Polk Street and was built in 1926. The long-serving spiritual leader was the beloved Rabbi Saul Silber. Today it is the home of the Seven Day Adventists, which means Sabbath services are still held on Saturday and the interior looks very much like it did the day the members of Anshe Sholom moved to the Lake View neighborhood. (Author's collection.)

The cornerstone here clearly states, in Hebrew and English, "Congregation Anshe Sholom." (Author's collection.)

Anshe Motele (men of Motele) was one of the oldest orthodox congregations in Chicago dating back to 1906. They built their Lawndale shul in 1928 at West Eighteenth Street and South Ridgeway Avenue. It later moved to the West Rogers Park community in 1956 during the "great" migration of the Jewish community. (Author's collection.)

In this more-recent photograph, after nearly 80 years, the name on the stone relief is still very visible. (Author's collection.)

Temple Judea, which was located at 1227 South Independence Boulevard, was the only reform congregation on the West Side. Their religious leaders were Rabbi George Zepin and Rabbi A. J. Messing. After closing in the 1950s, its name was acquired for a new reform congregation in Skokie. (Courtesy of *History of the Jews of Chicago*.)

Lawndale Conservative Synagogue was the only progressive conservative Jewish congregation on the West Side. It held its services at the Jewish Peoples Institute (JPI). (Courtesy of Trudy Levenstam Cooper and Saraine Levenstam Corn.)

Lawndale Conservative Synagogue

Rabbi Gershon G. Rosenstock

WILL CONDUCT

HIGH HOLIDAY SERVICES

ROSH HASHANAH
OCTOBER 3, 4 and 5

YOM KIPPUR
OCTOBER 12 and 13

Rabbi Rosenstock's inspiring leadership will assure meaningful, traditional services in Hebrew and English with stirring sermons on the burning issues of the day. Herold Lerner, outstanding young Cantor, will chant traditional melodies.

IN THE AUDITORIUM OF THE

Jewish Peoples Institute
2500 W. DOUGLAS BOULEVARD

Cantor Herold Lerner

The JPI was the leading cultural, social, and educational organization on the West Side. From nursery school to golden age groups, the JPI was the epicenter of cultural life in the Lawndale neighborhood. (Courtesy of the Jewish Community Centers of Metropolitan Chicago.)

A Purim festival costume party is seen here at the JPI around 1927. (Courtesy of the Jewish Community Centers of Metropolitan Chicago.)

Many plays and orchestrations were presented for the Lawndale community at the auditorium of the JPI. (Author's collection.)

The Star of David motif in the terrazzo floor of the lobby of the JPI can still be seen today. (Author's collection.)

The Hebrew Parochial School of the Jewish Peoples Institute graduating class of 1952 is pictured here. (Courtesy of Davina Packer Siegel.)

The Hebrew Theological College was the leading institution of Jewish culture and Hebrew education on the West Side. It was located at West Douglas Boulevard and South St. Louis Avenue. Many future Chicago rabbis received their early training here. (Courtesy of *History of the Jews of Chicago*.)

This postcard is from the 20th anniversary of the Hebrew Theological College. (Courtesy of Charlotte Kaplan.)

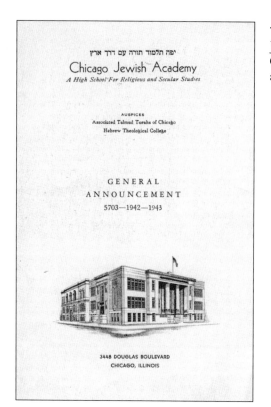

This is an announcement for the Chicago Jewish Academy from 1943. (Courtesy of Ida Crown Academy, Rabbi Leonard Matanky and Wendy Margolin.)

The student body of the Chicago Jewish Academy are seen here in the 1930s. (Courtesy of Ida Crown Academy and Rabbi Leonard Matanky.)

Marks Nathan Jewish Orphan Home was established on the Northwest Side in 1906. It later erected this new and enlarged facility in 1912. (Courtesy of *History of the Jews of Chicago*.)

This photograph is of residents of the Marks Nathan Jewish Orphan Home in 1915. (Courtesy of the Jewish Federation Collection.)

The Washington Boulevard Temple was the result of the merger of B'nai Abraham (1870) and Zion Temple (1885), which became B'nai Abraham Zion and was located at 25 North Karlov Avenue. The only known rendering is from Hyman L. Meites's *History of the Jews of Chicago.* Here one can see the program from the 1925 annual congregational meeting. Their long-serving rabbi was Samuel Schwartz and the renowned scholar Dr. Guenther Plaut. (Courtesy of Oak Park Temple/B'nai Abraham Zion.)

This is a photograph of the confirmation class of the Temple B'nai Abraham Zion in 1949. (Courtesy of Hannah Deitch.)

The Washington Boulevard Community House is seen here. (Author's collection.)

This stone lintel shows the name of the community house with the Star of David engraving. (Author's collection.)

This photograph shows the students of the Washington Boulevard Temple celebrating the holiday of Purim in the community house. (Courtesy of Hannah Deitch.)

Long demolished to make way for the Congress Expressway (now the Eisenhower), Congregation Hagro Anshe Wilno (men of the Vilna Goan [spiritual leader]) was located at 3901 West Congress Boulevard. Their rabbi was Solomon Zaiman. This is the only known photograph that shows the main sanctuary during the festival of Purim. (Courtesy of Naomi and Chester Gaines and Rita Stevens.)

Congregation B'nai Israel of Austin (children of Israel) was the leading conservative congregation in the Austin neighborhood, located at 5433 West Jackson Boulevard. Its first rabbi was Louis J. Lehrfeld, and its long-serving spiritual leaders were Rabbi Nachman Arnoff and Rabbi Shlomoh Z. Fineberg. (Author's collection.)

The Hebrew school of Congregation B'nai Israel of Austin was erected in 1949. (Author's collection.)

The Austin Jewish Community Center (traditional) was located at 116 South Central Avenue. Its longtime leader was Rabbi Louis J. Lehrfeld. (Author's collection.)

Anshe Shavel V Yanova (men of Shavel and Yanova)/Central Hebrew Congregation was located at 52 North Central Avenue in the Austin community. (Courtesy of Irving Cutler.)

Six

SOUTH SIDE

Temple KAM (congregation men of the west) is the oldest reform Jewish congregation in the city of Chicago, having been established in 1847. In 1874, they purchased a Plymouth church and converted it into a temple at East Twenty-sixth Street and South Indiana Avenue. Rabbi Leibman Adler was their long-serving spiritual leader. (Courtesy of *History of the Jews of Chicago.*)

Chicago Sinai Congregation is the oldest un-reconstituted reform congregation and dates to 1861 as a break-away group from KAM. In 1876, they purchased a Lutheran church and outfitted it as a temple. Its early rabbis were Bernhard Felsenthal, Isaac Chronic, and Kaufmann Kohler. It was located at East Twenty-first Street and South Indiana Avenue. (Courtesy of *History of the Jews of Chicago.*)

Rabbi Isaac Chronic was the leader of Chicago Sinai Congregation from 1864 to 1869. (Courtesy of Chicago Sinai Congregation.)

In 1892, the architectural firm of Adler and Sullivan remodeled the East Twenty-first Street location of Chicago Sinai Congregation. (Courtesy of Norman D. Schwartz.)

The venerable and beloved Rabbi Emil G. Hirsch was rabbi of Chicago Sinai Congregation from 1880 to 1923. (Courtesy of Chicago Sinai Congregation.)

Note the elegant design and fortresslike stonework that is reminiscent of the Adler and Sullivan auditorium building on the exterior of KAM. Also notice the stone lintel admonishing those who enter the "gates of righteousness." (Author's collection.)

The exterior of KAM after the disastrous fire of 2006 is seen here. The name in Hebrew on the stone lintel is still intact. (Author's collection.)

Isaiah Temple (reform) was the last building designed by Dankmar Adler before his death in 1900. It was located at East Forty-sixth Street and South Vincennes Avenue. The building's cornerstone was laid in the 1898, and the building was dedicated in 1899. (Author's collection.)

Isaiah Temple sold their Forty-sixth Street building to Ebenezer Missionary Baptist Church when it built its new Alfred Alshuler–designed temple at South Greenwood Avenue and East Hyde Park Boulevard. The cornerstone is still quite visible over a century later. (Author's collection.)

Temple B'nai Sholom (children of peace), begun in 1852, and Temple Israel, begun in 1898, merged to bring together two of the oldest reform congregations on the South Side. In 1913, they erected this magnificent edifice designed by the renowned architect Alfred Alschuler. (Author's collection.)

Kehilath Anshe Dorum (congregation men of the South Side) was located at East Fifty-ninth Street and South Michigan Avenue. It was built in 1915; the only remaining structure is the Hebrew school on the left of the photograph. (Courtesy of *History of the Jews of Chicago*.)

A. D. Beth Hamidrash Hagodol, 1912, was located at East Fifty-ninth Street and South Indiana Avenue. (Courtesy of *History of the Jews of Chicago*.)

The stone lintel of A. D. Beth Hamidrash Hagodol is pictured here. (Author's collection.)

Chicago Sinai Congregation, 1912, located at Grand Boulevard at East Forty-sixth Street, is a classic design of architect Alfred Alschuler. Its long beloved rabbi was Dr. Emil G. Hirsch who served for over 40 years. (Courtesy of Chicago Sinai Congregation.)

People celebrate the armistice of 1918 for World War I. (Courtesy of Chicago Sinai Congregation.)

In 1924, Chicago's oldest temple, KAM, built its final independent structure. It was designed by the architectural firm of Newhouse and Bernham in the Greek Revival style and was located at South Drexel Boulevard and East Fiftieth Street. Its long beloved spiritual leader was Rabbi Jacob Weinstein. The building is the current home of the Operation Push Rainbow Coalition. (Courtesy of *History of the Jews of Chicago*.)

The 1944 confirmation class of KAM is seen here. (Courtesy of Barbara Chester.)

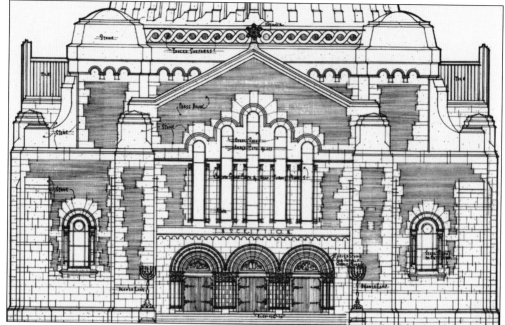

Rodfei Zedek had outgrown their East Forty-eighth Street building and decided to move to the more fashionable Hyde Park neighborhood. They hired well-known architect Abraham Epstein to design a magnificent edifice to occupy. In 1924, the selection committee approved the very elaborate design, but after much discussion among the board and membership, it was decided that this building would be too expensive for the congregation. This rendering is of the front view, facing South Greenwood Avenue. (Courtesy of Sidney and Raymond Epstein.)

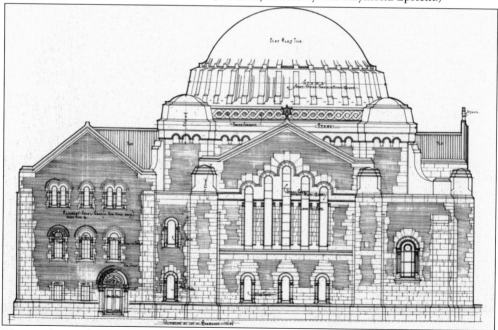

This rendering shows the East Fifty-fourth Place side of the proposed synagogue. (Courtesy of Sidney and Raymond Epstein.)

106

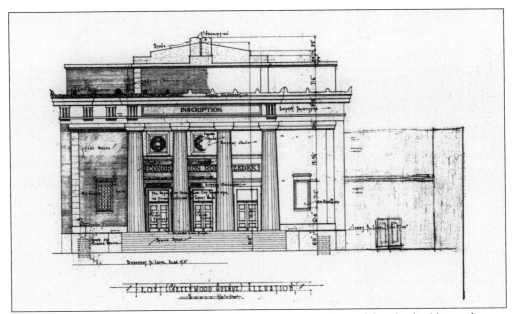

Finally, this rendering of a more classical structure was approved by the building selection committee and the entire congregation. This rendering is of the Greenwood Avenue front entrance to the building. (Courtesy of Sidney and Raymond Epstein.)

This photograph shows the completed Congregation Rodfei Zedek. (Courtesy of Congregation Rodfei Zedek.)

CHICAGO
SINAI
CONGREGATION

Dedication

THE NEW TEMPLE
AND RELIGIOUS SCHOOL

MARCH THIRD, FOURTH AND FIFTH
NINETEEN HUNDRED FIFTY

This is a dedication booklet of Chicago Sinai Congregation's new Hyde Park temple in 1950. The building was designed by the architectural firm of Friedman, Alschuler and Sincere. (Courtesy of Elaine Kaplan.)

Shown here is a 1950 groundbreaking ceremony for the new Chicago Sinai Congregation, located at South Shore Drive. Rabbi Louis Mann (second from left) is seen dedicating the land. (Courtesy of Chicago Sinai Congregation.)

Chicago Sinai Congregation's last South Side location on South South Shore Drive was dedicated in 1950. It is the oldest classic reform temple in Chicago. Its long-serving spiritual leader was the venerable Rabbi Dr. Louis Mann who served for nearly 40 years. (Courtesy of Steve Grubman.)

Beth Hamedrosh Hagodol Anshe Dorum (house of great study South Side), also known as Rabbi Eleazer Mushkin's shul, was the oldest independent orthodox congregation on the South Side. Mushkin had been the spiritual leader of this synagogue for the last 30 years of its existence. The building was later sold to Elijah Mohammed in 1954 as the first black Muslim mosque in Chicago. After selling its beloved synagogue, Beth Hamedrosh Hagodol merged with Congregation Kehilath Israel on East Ninety-ninth Street. (Courtesy of Irving Cutler.)

This 1940s etching is of Congregation Oir Chodosh (new light), which was established in the Englewood neighborhood in the early 1900s for the benefit of the Jewish merchants who chose to live in the community. Early on, it was a progressive conservative congregation. (Courtesy of Norman D. Schwartz.)

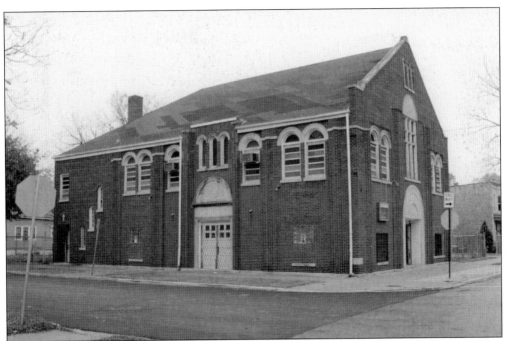

Congregation Anshey Emeth (men of truth) was located at West Sixty-second and South May Streets in the Englewood neighborhood. The Englewood community was small, made up of mostly Jewish shopkeepers and businessman. (Author's collection.)

The stone door lintel of Congregation Anshey Emeth of Englewood is still visible nearly 90 years after its construction. (Author's collection.)

B'nai Israel of Englewood/First Englewood Congregation, located at West Sixty-second Street and South Aberdeen Street, or "the Aberdeen Avenue shul" was constructed in 1911. The spiritual leader was Rabbi E. Samuel Ramirovsky. (Author's collection.)

This beautiful stained-glass Star of David is still visible at the rear of the women's balcony. This being an orthodox synagogue, there was a separate women's area in the upper balcony for the women of First Englewood. (Author's collection.)

The Chicago Home for Jewish Orphans was located at South Drexel Avenue and East Sixty-second Street. The first orphan home for Jewish children in Chicago was established in 1899. (Courtesy of the Joan and Jerome Drapekin Collection, the Chicago Jewish Archives and the Spertus College of Judaica.)

The children's band of the Chicago Home for Jewish Orphans is pictured here around 1910. (Courtesy of the Joan and Jerome Drapekin Collection, the Chicago Jewish Archives and the Spertus College of Judaica.)

Beth Am (peoples house) was located at East Seventy-first Street and South Coles Avenue. This reform congregation served the South Shore community for many years until the change of residents and safety caused the membership to decline. The cornerstone was set in 1956 and the dedication was in 1957. The congregation's spiritual leader was Rabbi Eric Friedland. (Courtesy of Irving Cutler.)

South Shore Temple, located at 7215 South Jeffrey Boulevard, was one of the leading reform congregations in the South Shore neighborhood and was organized in 1922 and set about immediately to build a Hebrew school and community center. Later they were able to build their modern temple in 1952. Its long-serving religious leaders were Rabbi George Fox and Rabbi Ahron Opher. In the 1970s, South Shore Temple membership sold their building to Landmark Church due to the changing demographics of the South Shore community. (Courtesy of Irving Cutler.)

The corner of East Seventy-sixth Street and South Philips Avenue was a main intersection in the South Shore neighborhood. Seen here, Congregation Habonim (builders), a conservative congregation, was established by German Jewish refugees from Germany in the late 1940s. Habonim was built in the early 1950s. (Author's collection.)

Congregation B'nai Bezalel (children in the image of God) was established in the Woodlawn community in 1904. After leaving their longtime (since 1928) neighborhood location at East Sixtieth Street and South Champlain Avenue, they relocated to the growing and younger South Shore community and erected their synagogue just across the street from Congregation Habonim in 1955. Rabbi Abraham Shoulson led this conservative congregation for many years. (Author's collection.)

Southside Hebrew Congregation is the oldest progressive conservative Jewish synagogue in the South Shore neighborhood, having been established at South Indiana Avenue and East Thirty-fifth Street in 1901. It was located at East Seventy-fourth Street and South Chappel Avenue and built in 1927, designed by architect Morris L. Komar. When South Side Hebrew moved to the new location on Chappel, they combined with two other local synagogues, Ohavei Emunah (lovers of faith) and Etz Hayyim (land of life). The spiritual leaders were Rabbi Teller and Rabbi Maurice Kliers. (Author's collection.)

The front entrance stone lintel reveals the merging of three South Side congregations to make up South Side Hebrew Congregation. The two others were Ohavei Emunah (lovers of faith) and Etz Hayyim (land of life). (Author's collection.)

The confirmation class of Southside Hebrew Congregation poses here in 1947. Rabbi Teller is also pictured. (Courtesy of Sarane Meyer.)

SS HEBREW CONG SCHOOL GIMEL-ALEPH I NOV 1959

The school class of Southside Hebrew Congregation is seen in this 1959 photograph. (Courtesy of Charlotte Kaplan.)

The Young Men's Jewish Council was located at East Seventy-sixth Street and South Philips Avenue and was the center of youth activity for the South Shore community. (Author's collection.)

Boy Scouts were an integral part of all the Jewish congregations. Here a group of Scouts from several Chicago area synagogues can be seen. (Courtesy of Charlotte Kaplan.)

The largest Jewish community center in the South Shore community was the South Side Center, later Henry Hart Jewish Community Center, which was located at East Ninety-first Street and South Jeffery Avenue. It was built in 1960. (Author's collection.)

The Henry Hart Jewish Community Center had many programs for the areas youth. The summer day campers are seen here in 1966. (Courtesy of Sheryl Zisook Schneider.)

Congregation Agudath Achim South Shore, located at 7933 South Yates Avenue, was the first synagogue to be built after World War II. The cornerstone was laid in 1948, and the dedication was in 1949. The longtime spiritual leader was Rabbi Harold P. Smith. (Author's collection.)

Here is Agudath Achim South Shore as it is today, the new Nazareth Methodist Baptist Church. Still visible is the cornerstone with the English and Hebrew dates; 5708 and 1948. (Author's collection.)

Congregation Bikur Cholim (visitors of the sick) later merged with Agudath Achim South Shore (society of brothers) in the 1970s and was the longest-serving Jewish congregation and synagogue (from 1898 and 1902 until 2003) in the city of Chicago. The congregation's spiritual leader was Rabbi Hirsh Harrison. It later became home to Chicago's oldest black Hebrew congregation, Beth Shalom B'nai Zaken whose rabbi is Funnye Capers. (Author's collection.)

A rare photograph of the interior of Congregation Bikur Cholim Agudath Achim located at 8729 South Houston Avenue, this image was taken in the 1960s. (Courtesy of Irving Cutler.)

Congregation Kehilath Israel (Congregation Israel) was located at 2349 East Ninety-ninth Street in the Merionette Manor and Jeffrey Manor neighborhoods and was built in 1953. Its long-serving spiritual leader was the beloved Rabbi Eliot Einhorn. (Courtesy of Mort Einhorn.)

Seen here is Rabbi Eliot Einhorn with a bar mitzvah boy on his special day at Congregation Kehilath Israel in the mid-1950s. (Courtesy of Mort Einhorn.)

The cornerstone is being set at Congregation Kehilath Israel in 1953 in this photograph. (Courtesy of Mort Einhorn.)

This photograph shows the giving of the blessings for the new Congregation Kehilath Israel by Rabbi Eliot Einhorn. (Courtesy of Mort Einhorn.)

The last South Side location of Anshe Kanesses Israel, the Russiche shul, was at East Seventy-fifth Street and South Yates Boulevard and was built about 1954. Still visible are the inlaid menorahs on the brick facade. (Author's collection.)

Temple B'nai Yehuda was built in 1959–1960 and was located at East Eightieth Street and South Jeffery Boulevard. Known as the "Teepee Temple" after its design, it was the first permanent location of Hyde Park liberal congregation. Their spiritual leader was Rabbi Malcolm Irving Cohen. (Courtesy of Irving Cutler.)

The farthest south one can go in Chicago is the community of Roseland. Here is the Congregation Shomre Hadas (keepers of the faith) located at 11445 South Forest Avenue. The synagogue was dedicated just before the Great Depression in 1929. Their spiritual leader was Rabbi Gershon G. Rosenstock. (Author's collection.)

The cornerstone of Congregation Shomre Hadas shows the Hebrew date of 5689, which corresponds to 1928. Even after nearly 80 years, the date is still visible. (Author's collection.)

Lawn Manor Community Center, one of only two Jewish congregations on the Southwest Side, was located at West Sixty-sixth Street and South Troy Street and was built in 1925. The congregation's beloved spiritual leader was Rabbi Mordechai Schultz. It was the leading synagogue congregation on the Southwest Side. (Author's collection.)

This photograph shows the interior of the old Lawn Manor Community Center sanctuary and confirmation classes before the renovation. (Courtesy of Ruth Schultz Hecktman.)

Lawn Manor Congregation, later Lawn Manor Beth Jacob after the merger in the 1970s with Beth Jacob of Scottsdale located at West Sixty-seventh Street and South Kedzie Avenue, was built in 1952. The spiritual leader after the retirement of Rabbi Mordechai Schultz was Rabbi David Tamarkin. It was later sold to the black Hebrew congregation Beth Shalom B'nai Zaken in 2003, which had sold its South East Side building, located at East Eighty-seventh Street and South Houston Avenue. (Author's collection.)

Rabbi Schultz is seen here, second from left. in the new Lawn Manor Hebrew Congregation during the High Holidays. Here is "Blowing the Shofar" to welcome in the Jewish new year. The year is 1956. (Courtesy of Ruth Schults Hecktman.)

ACROSS AMERICA, PEOPLE ARE DISCOVERING SOMETHING WONDERFUL. THEIR HERITAGE.

Arcadia Publishing is the leading local history publisher in the United States. With more than 3,000 titles in print and hundreds of new titles released every year, Arcadia has extensive specialized experience chronicling the history of communities and celebrating America's hidden stories, bringing to life the people, places, and events from the past. To discover the history of other communities across the nation, please visit:

www.arcadiapublishing.com

Customized search tools allow you to find regional history books about the town where you grew up, the cities where your friends and family live, the town where your parents met, or even that retirement spot you've been dreaming about.